101 ESSENTIAL LISTS
FOR THE EARLY
YEARS

Penny Tassoni

continuum
LONDON • NEW YORK

Continuum International Publishing Group
The Tower Building   80 Maiden Lane
11 York Road   Suite 704
London   New York
SE1 7NX   NY 10038

www.continuumbooks.com

© Penny Tassoni 2006

British Library Cataloguing-in-Publication Data
A catalogue record for this book is available from the British Library.

ISBN: 0–8264–8863–3 (paperback)

Library of Congress Cataloging-in-Publication Data
A catalog record for this book is available from the Library of Congress.

Typeset by YHT Ltd
Printed and bound in Great Britain by Ashford Colour Press Ltd, Gosport, Hampshire

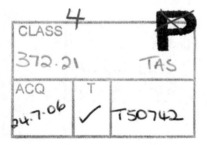

CONTENTS

Starting Out

L I S T 1   Reasons to work with children

○ It's not boring – the job may be demanding and tiring, but there's always something happening.

○ You might make a difference – children are heavily influenced by who they are with. Your interest and care is making a difference.

○ It's fun – if you provide interesting activities and actually join in with them, you will enjoy yourself. What other job allows you to play with sand, water and dough, as well as do some dressing up?

○ You face and survive challenges – cleaning up grazes, coping with anxious parents and separating brawling children are all just part of the job!

○ The laughter and smiles keep coming – it takes relatively little to impress young children, and the beam of a toddler is worth getting up for!

○ There are huge opportunities within the sector – it's easy to move jobs and change direction.

○ It's a job where you are constantly learning – new initiatives, new children and new parents.

LIST 2

Your essential kit

There are some things you need to have handy when working with children. One minute you might be wiping a nose, another you might be writing a message to a parent.

For accidents, snotty noses and sticky hands

- Tissues or toilet roll
- Wipes
- Plastic bags
- Cloth
- Accident book
- Disposable gloves
- First-aid kit.

For practical activities

- Sticky tape, masking tape and scissors
- Pencil, felt-tip pens
- Pritt-style glue
- Eraser, ruler and pencil sharpener
- Teddy, puppet or cuddly toy
- Apron.

For observations and quick notes to parents

- Pen
- Notepad
- Digital camera (providing that consent has been obtained from parents beforehand).

Bits and bobs

- Swiss Army Knife with a screwdriver – keep it tucked away in a handbag or cupboard.
- Finger puppet – comes in handy when comforting children who have had an accident, or 'wobbly' new children.
- Dance tape or CD – always useful for wet days and long afternoons.

Jobs for first thing in the morning

Getting organized first thing in the morning can make a difference to the rest of the day. If you have any students or helpers, give them this list too!

- Put on some music.
- Open a window slightly.
- Look at the planner while it's quiet. Prepare any paperwork for helpers, letters for parents, etc.
- Fill the water tray and put out the toys.
- Rake and sieve the sand. Put out the toys. Check that the dustpan and brush are out.
- Put out the dough or make fresh dough. Put out the toys.
- Set out the role-play area, with props. Hang up any garments.
- Lay out three or four jigsaws on a table, and start to make one of them.
- Prepare the painting area. Put out paper, paints and brushes. Check that a cloth is available.
- Check that aprons are available for paint, sand and water.
- Arrange the book corner. Put some books on display and plump up the cushions.
- Set out the collage and writing areas. Put out fresh glue, spreaders, paper and a range of materials.
- Get out the construction toys and maybe begin making something for the children to finish.
- Put out some types of small world play, e.g. a train set, farm animals, doll's house.
- Prepare other planned activities.
- Go outside and check for litter, damage or animal mess.
- Once back inside, check the toilet area.
- Breathe deeply, relax and start the day with a smile!

Making your life easier

Working with children can be stressful and demanding, so it's essential to find ways of reducing the hassle factor.

Be organized!

○ Try and be as tidy as possible and encourage children to be too!
○ Use labels, lists and noticeboards.
○ Store planning notes on a computer so that you can tweak them for another year.

Accept help

○ Make it a priority to get volunteers in to help.
○ Give volunteers fulfilling tasks.
○ Develop their expertise in dealing with particular activities or children.
○ Make sure that other people understand the way you have organized the room and set things out.
○ Teach children how to put out equipment and to set up activities. Time spent teaching them how to be self-reliant will be paid back in bucket loads.

Pace yourself

○ Think about the hassle factor involved in activities. Make sure that you have a mix of 'low' and 'high hassle' activities.
○ When you're doing your long-term planning, think about how tired you (and the children) might be at certain points in the term.
○ Make sure that you build in enough time to have a proper break each day. Be still and quiet and take the time to recharge a little.
○ Finally, remember that you don't have to be perfect. The world will not end because the dough is too sticky!

LIST 5   Things that can go wrong

Life is full of mishaps. Try and avoid some of these though!

- Someone forgets to get the snacks in.
- The cleaner walks out.
- The cook walks out.
- A child who is not allowed cake manages to get hold of some.
- You can't remember where you have put the cheque that a parent has given you.
- An accident slip is left in the office rather than sent home with the child.
- At parents' evening you start talking about the wrong child.
- You forget to lock up, but remember when you are just about to go to bed.
- You lose a toy that a child has brought in and it turns out to be a family heirloom.
- A child is sent home with the wrong person.
- A child goes on a walkabout and no one notices for two hours.

L I S T 6 Confidentiality and data protection

During the course of your job, you are bound to pick up lots of snippets of information. Disclosing some of this information to others, even innocently, can ruin a career.

- Try and see any information that you gain about children and their families, as well as colleagues, as being privileged. It should only be shared with others who have a similar status and even then only if it is in the child's interests.
- Don't agree to keep information confidential if you know that this is not possible, e.g. a parent tells you that their partner has hit the child.
- Don't gossip about children or their families – be particularly careful in the staffroom, even though other colleagues might not be so restrained.
- Think carefully about what you say to helpers and visitors about the children you work with. Comments have been known to find their way back to parents, e.g. 'he's spoilt rotten at home'!

Data Protection Act

This Act covers written personal information and is no longer just about what is stored on computers. You have a duty to keep information confidential and secure. Find out more by visiting the Information Commissioner's Office website (www.dataprotection.gov.uk).

Websites, books and magazines

Look out for the following resources.

Early years magazines

- *Nursery World*
- *Early Years Educator*
- *Practical Childcare*

Key curriculum documents

- England
  - *Birth to Three Matters*
  (available from the DfES publication department at www.dfes.gov.uk).
  - *Curriculum Guidance for the Foundation Stage*
  (available from QCA, www.qca.org.uk).
- Scotland
  - *Birth to Three: supporting our youngest children*
  - *A Curriculum Framework for Children 3–5*
  (available from www.ltscotland.org.uk).
- Wales
  - *Desirable Outcomes for Children's Learning before Compulsory School Age*
  (available from www.accac.org.uk).
- Northern Ireland
  Look out for the conclusion to the review of pre-school education (www.deni.gov.uk).

Books with ideas and activities

- *The Little Book* series by Sally Featherstone
- *Planning Play and the Early Years* by Penny Tassoni and Karen Hucker (Heinemann)
- *Planning for the Foundation Stage: Ideas for Themes and Activities* by Penny Tassoni (Heinemann).

Books for managers

- *7 Habits of Highly Effective People* by Stephen Covey (Simon & Schuster).

Websites

- www.dfes.gov.uk
- www.surestart.gov.uk
- www.ltscotland.org.uk/earlyyears
- www.bookstart.org.uk.

Layout and Organization

2

LIST 8 Getting a good routine

Children respond well to a good routine, so it's worth taking time out to check that the routine that is in place is working well.

There are some telltale signs that your routine has reached its sell-by date.

- You dread a certain part of the day.
- You frequently feel in a rush and not on top of things.
- There are regular times when children are wandering around.
- The same types of inappropriate behaviour are shown at the same times each day, e.g. children pushing each other or whinging.
- There never seems enough time to have fun.

Make a list of everything that happens during the session or day.

- How long does it take?
- How well do children respond?
- How easy is it for adults to manage?
- What is its purpose?
- Who benefits from it?
- Does it have to happen at that time?

Now it's time to make some changes to the routine.

- Ditch anything that seems pointless.
- Focus on ways of keeping children playing and being busy for as long as possible.
- Cut down the time spent on boring bits of the session, e.g. getting coats, going to the toilet. This usually involves getting smaller groups of children to do things at a time.
- Be creative and more flexible – if large-group story time is not working, think about having a story time as a small-group activity.

Morning and home time

- Wear an apron with a pocket so that odd objects, accident slips and letters from parents aren't forgotten.
- If the cloakroom area is small and gets crowded, provide coat hangers so that coats can be sorted out in the room.
- Timing and organization are often the keys to avoiding situations where parents are waiting restlessly and you are rushing around trying to finish off activities or stuff letters into envelopes.

In the morning

- Try and get in early or leave everything ready the night before.
- Spot parents or children who look anxious, and make a pre-emptive strike!
- Put out play materials that will tempt children and help them to settle.
- Have a pad ready so that you don't forget any information that parents give you, such as who is picking the child up.
- Smile!

At home time

- Wear a digital watch and set it to beep half an hour before the end of the session.
- Put named carrier bags with children's bits and pieces in them onto their coatpegs so that letters, artwork, comforters, etc. don't get lost.
- Remember that once toys and equipment have been tidied up, children will be at a loose end. Keep out some activities or develop a toy box with bits and pieces that are only used at the end of the day. This works well if children are collected at different times.
- Make sure that you are available to talk to parents – remember to hand out personally any accident slips.
- Keep an eye out for children, especially toddlers, who try and slip out unaccompanied.

LIST 10   Managing snacks and toilets

Snack time and toilets are points in the day when chaos can easily break out.

Snacks

Think about how best to organise snack times. Do children have to be fed all together or can you try one of these ideas?

- Children come up during the session and serve themselves. They post their name so that staff can check who has been. Water is also available in this area at all times.
- Snack time is seen as a small group activity. Children prepare their fruit snack together. This is a fantastic way of meeting loads of learning outcomes.
- Combine story and snack time. Small groups of children have something to eat and drink while you provide 'live entertainment' by reading a story.
- Give children who have not had much breakfast an 'early' snack. Lack of food and drink in the morning affects concentration and behaviour!

Toilets

Toilets can be a source of worry for young children! Toilet time can also be a dreaded moment for the adults too!

- Where possible, ensure that children have access to toilets when they need them.
- Where children need to be supervised, take them in small groups to avoid a constant 'drip' of children needing to go. Advertise the fact that you are doing a toilet run!
- Make sure that the toilets smell nice and that there is plenty of soap and paper towels.
- Be matter of fact about the whole process and remember that children need their privacy.
- Praise children who remember automatically to wash their hands.

LIST 11   Encouraging healthy eating

With obesity in children hitting all time high levels, healthy eating is on people's minds. So what can we give children to eat?

For young children, healthy eating is about enjoying food, learning about new tastes, but also getting 'nutrient-rich' food. This means food that contains vitamins and minerals as well as proteins, carbohydrates and fat. Overweight children are likely to have diets that lack sufficient fresh fruit and vegetables but are high on processed foods which tend to be calorie-rich rather than nutrient-rich.

○ Make sure that food is tasty! Children like fast food because it often has strong flavours.
○ Encourage children to be involved in the preparation of food – chopping up fruit, grating cheese.
○ As soon as possible, allow children to serve themselves. This helps them to learn about how much they need.
○ Cook from scratch as much as possible, using fresh fruit and vegetables.
○ Avoid making eating into a competition as to who can clear their plate first or have second helpings.
○ Make sure that puddings are seen as part of the meal rather than as rewards.

Snacks

Young children's stomachs cannot take in sufficient food on just three meals a day.

Snacks should be seen as part of the child's overall diet, providing opportunities for nutrients.

○ Make sure that they are not so filling that children do not eat their main meals.
○ Avoid snacks that are processed, such as crisps and biscuits. These are nutrient-poor as they lack vitamins and protein and simply fill children up.
○ Always make sure that children have access to water.

Try some of these:

o popped corn (in the microwave)
o cheese and crackers
o chopped raw vegetables and dips
o dried-fruit mix: raisins, sultanas, dried apricots
o fresh fruit: melon cubes, pineapple cubes, apples, bananas, orange slices.

Drinks

o Water with slices of lemon and ice cubes
o Yoghurt drink
o Milkshakes
o Fruit juice cocktails.

For more information about healthy eating for young children, consider buying *Eating well for under 5s in child care*, published by the Caroline Walker Trust (www.cwt.org.uk).

LIST 12 Getting children to do some of the work

Persuading the children to help is essential if you are to keep sane and manage your workload. Inspectors will also be looking out for the way in which children are given independence and responsibility.

○ See tidying, setting out and even the odd spot of cleaning as part of the curriculum. Put it in your planning.

○ Put out of reach anything that is fragile, dangerous or extremely messy.

○ De-clutter cupboards and storage areas so that children can see where things go. Be ruthless!

○ Less is more – have three small boxes of bricks rather than one enormous one that can be tipped over.

○ Do not set out everything in the room. Ask children to get out what they think they will need and make them responsible for putting it back.

○ Keep storage boxes small so that children can lift them in and out.

○ Label or use photographs or pictures on drawers and cupboards so that children know where things are kept.

○ Create teams of children for tidying up at the end of sessions – focus each team on a particular area of the room to avoid children running wild and messing around.

○ Encourage the older children in the room to help the younger ones.

○ Be patient, allow children time.

○ Keep instructions and tasks small.

○ Praise, praise and bribe with the odd sticker.

Ordering toys and equipment

Budgets are always tight, so make sure that you order what you really need. Begin by looking at your current provision and think about what really needs replacing, extending or refreshing. Some toy manufacturers will send out missing pieces for popular toys (e.g. odd pieces of games and puzzles) if you contact them.

When ordering new equipment, ask:

- ○ what will the children really get from it?
- ○ how many children at a time will be able to use it?
- ○ how easy will it be to store?
- ○ what will the hassle factor be like in supervising it and getting it out?
- ○ does it need batteries or any maintenance?

Educational suppliers are not always the best sources for some items. Always check out the local high street, especially the 'pound' shops. Avoid expensive art materials – young children need quantity as much as quality so that they can explore and have several attempts at something. Precious art stuff is likely to be rationed.

Safety

- ○ Always use and follow manufacturers' instructions.
- ○ Be careful about accepting second-hand toys and equipment. Anything electrical or with moving parts, such as a tricycle, needs to be checked carefully.
- ○ Check that new toys carry the Lion Mark. Note that the CE mark does not mean that the product has actually been tested for safety.

Providing varied opportunities

Learning through play means that we must put out varied resources for children. Observe what children usually play with and how long they stay there. Throw out, or at least re-formulate, anything that fails to attract them.

Sensory opportunities

○ Make sure that you put out plenty of sensory materials, such as sand, water and dough. They may be messy, but children are drawn to them like bees to honey!

○ Increase your provision by putting out small trays, such as cat-litter trays, with dry rice, bark chippings and even tea leaves.

Imaginative play

○ Remember to plan for small-world play as well as role-play.

○ Take imaginative play outside.

○ Increase play opportunities by bringing in other materials, e.g. dough into the kitchen or a tray of moss and leaves next to the farm animals.

Construction play

○ Think jigsaws, junk modelling as well as Duplo, Lego and large wooden bricks.

○ Encourage children to bring into this type of play cuddly toys, dinosaurs and play people, and don't forget to take it outdoors too!

LIST 15   The sand tray

Sand play is wonderful for children. It helps build fine and gross motor skills, as well as giving children first-hand experience of size, volume and texture.

Practical tips

- ❍ Make sure you have a dustpan and brush to hand or try letting the children use a handheld vacuum cleaner.
- ❍ Vary the way in which sand is presented. Try beginning the session with a 'mountain' of sand or with the sand being slightly damp.
- ❍ Use cat-litter trays or other containers to provide small-scale sand experiences for children.
- ❍ Use builders' mixing trays when you want to put the sand on the floor.
- ❍ From time to time, be ruthless and throw out sand toys that have faded or are very scratched.

Items to hide in the sand tray

(Store these in labelled ice cream tubs)

- ❍ Shells.
- ❍ Keys.
- ❍ Fake jewellery and coins.
- ❍ Farm animals and toy dinosaurs.
- ❍ Magnetic letters and numbers.

Traditional sand toys

- ❍ Sieves – also try tea-strainers.
- ❍ Bottles – use different shapes and sizes.
- ❍ Digging implements – try spoons.
- ❍ Buckets and containers.

New things to try

- ❍ Knives and forks – children can make sand pies and enjoy the sensation of cutting into them.
- ❍ Tubes and pipes – children can watch sand flowing.
- ❍ Put different lengths of straws poking up – see who can pull out the shortest straw!

The water tray

Water trays are traditional play items for young children. They help children to learn about volume and capacity, as well as building hand–eye coordination and fine motor skills.

Practical tips

- Never leave children unsupervised near water.
- Provide rain ponchos for very young children or your real splashers!
- Have towels and cloths to hand.
- Water can be slippery, so mop up any spills straight away.
- Take water outdoors – in builders' trays or paddling pools – but tip the water out at the end of the activity.
- Remember, big buckets result in big splashes!

Traditional water toys

- Boats and other objects that float.
- Buckets, bottles and other containers.
- Tubes and pipes.
- Toy watering cans, teapots, jugs.
- Rubber ducks and other plastic toys, including play people.

New things to try

- Ping-pong balls – they bounce straight up.
- Chinese water flowers – put them in small trays and watch them 'grow'.
- Wind-up water toys – children love these.
- Coloured ice cubes or 'hands' (water frozen inside rubber gloves).
- Wishing wells – see if children can drop a coin on top of one already at the bottom.
- Messages in bottles.

The dough table

Children love playing with dough. It is an easy activity to provide and can keep them playing and concentrating for some time. It also builds their fine motor movements and hand–eye coordination and gives them a sense of power!

Practical tips

○ Avoid putting a mountain of dough on a table – the first child there will take it all and then get upset when she/he has to share.
○ Put out place mats or even individual boxes or pots of dough so that children know how much is theirs.
○ If dough gets on the carpet, leave it to dry out completely. Scrape off the worst, vacuum and then, if required, use a dry, stiff brush.
○ Provide cling film or plastic gloves for those children who do not like getting their hands sticky or who have eczema.

Traditional toys

○ Cutters and rolling pins
○ Knives and modelling tools
○ Plates, cups and baking trays

New things to try

○ Put out scissors with dough – children can practise their scissor skills.
○ Make stretchy dough with the children – just mix together self-raising flour, food colouring and water.
○ Warm up the dough in the microwave on a cold day.

The role-play area

From around 18 months, children begin to enjoy pretend- or role-play. Role-play encourages children's language and social skills. Watch them as they immerse themselves in a fantasy land!

Practical tips

○ Less is more – too many clothes and props can result in a big mess.
○ If you have limited space for dressing-up clothes, use boxes for different types of props – shoes, scarves, kitchen utensils, jewellery.
○ Encourage children to plan their play – ask them what they will need out.
○ Have a good sort out and get rid of clothes or props that are unattractive.
○ Let children develop their play by allowing them to bring food into the home corner or have their snacks there.

Traditional resources

○ Tea set and kitchen utensils.
○ Dressing-up clothes.
○ Mirror.
○ Pushchairs and prams.
○ Cuddly toys.
○ Cash till, shopping baskets, packages and cans.

New things to try

○ Den-making outdoors – provide sheets of fabrics and pegs or pop-up tents.
○ Create a garden centre.
○ Create a fast food restaurant.
○ Create a baby clinic.
○ Holiday time – provide suitcases on wheels.

LIST 19 The construction area

Children enjoy putting things together. This type of play builds plenty of skills, including fine and gross motor movements.

Practical tips

○ Vary the opportunities – avoid having the same old toys out each time.
○ Make sure that there is sufficient floor space – the children will need to spill out.
○ Consider taking play outdoors – children love using large wooden blocks to supplement their play.
○ Look out for toys that are wooden as they have an extra tactile dimension.
○ Supplement this type of play with small-world equipment, such as farm animals that can wander onto the train tracks!

Types of toys and equipment

○ Large and small wooden blocks
○ Lego and Duplo
○ Train sets – the wooden ones are usually favoured by children
○ Jigsaws – large floor ones, as well as smaller wooden ones
○ Quadro – large apparatus that interconnects and can be used to build houses and climbing frames
○ Modelling sets – some simple kits are available
○ Marble runs

Home made construction!

○ Be bold and bring in materials that children can use for their own creations.
○ Look out for drainpipes, off-cuts of wood and large-scale junk such as cardboard boxes and plastic crates. This can be far more fun than using 'educational' toys.

L I S T 20   Coping with paint

Painting can be done more easily if we provide large areas for children. It means that they do not run out of paper all the time. It also helps to develop their gross motor skills.

Creating a painting wall

○ Put up a shower curtain or a sheet of thick plastic with masking tape.
○ Place large sheets of paper on it, again using masking tape.
○ Make it look smarter by trimming the edge with tinsel!

Using the painting wall

○ Put aprons on (or rain ponchos for the really messy!).
○ Give each child a polystyrene tray with the primary colours and white on it. This eliminates the need for paint pots and prevents them from overloading their brushes.
○ Give each child a large paintbrush – think about buying in cheap decorating brushes.
○ Let children paint side-by-side or by themselves.
○ Mark out their area of the painting wall.
○ Do some painting yourself – this is the greatest way of encouraging children to paint.
○ If you do not have a sink nearby, place some soapy water and a cloth near the wall.
○ Afterwards, make sure that the children wash their own brushes. The trays can be thrown away or easily wiped under a running tap.

Organizing outdoor play

Children love being outdoors. It's full of play and learning possibilities if you can get the practical organization right.

Coping with the weather

○ Children are less put off by rain and wind than adults.

○ Buy a set of rain ponchos that children can slip on easily. Hang them up by the door and make sure that you have an adult-sized one too!

○ Provide a box of wellingtons so that children can go out splashing.

○ Put out cardboard boxes and fabrics so that children can make their own dens and shelters if it is hot and sunny.

○ Look out for large free-standing parasols or sheets of thin fabric that you can use to make shelters.

○ Have some spare long-sleeved t-shirts and some caps in case children have forgotten theirs.

Storage

○ Look out for stackable storage boxes with lids that can be used outdoors. Recycling bins are good for this.

○ Work hard to get an outdoor shed, but make sure that it has double doors so that it is easy to get equipment in and out.

Going on outings

Outings are hard work to organize, but are enriching experiences for children. Think carefully about where you are going before making any arrangements and always check out the location in person. Ask yourself some key questions:

- What will the children gain from the visit?
- What will it be like if it rains or is cold?
- How easy will it be to manage groups of children?
- What are the health and safety considerations?
- How long will it take to go round or do the activities?
- How helpful are the staff?
- How good are the toilet facilities?
- Where will you eat?

Tips for a smooth trip

- Avoid Mondays – you'll only spend the weekend thinking about it!
- Allow a contingency fund when working out the cost, which might include refunds for children who are ill on the day.
- Check out the insurance angle.
- Remember to get updated medical and emergency details from parents, as well as signed consent forms.
- Confirm the coach and venue booking in writing.
- Phone again to double check a couple of days before the trip.
- Work out how you will manage:
  - children being sick on the day
  - children disappearing
  - helpers disappearing
  - rain, wind, snow or extreme heat
  - coaches or trains being delayed or not turning up.

What to take with you on the day

- A charged mobile phone.
- Plenty of spare change and a tip for the driver.
- A first-aid kit, sun lotion and sick bucket.
- Bottles of water and spare food.
- A change of clothes, including knickers, a raincoat and sun hat.

- Toilet paper, plenty of tissues and wipes.
- Written instructions and registers for helpers.
- Black bags and some carrier bags.
- A Swiss Army Knife with scissors and screwdriver (comes in very handy).

Planning

L I S T 23 Getting down to planning

The word planning is often accompanied by a large groan, but planning is an essential part of the job.

Reasons why you need to plan

- It will make your life easier – both you and the children will know what to do!
- It makes a difference to children's behaviour – they do not become bored.
- It is part of the inspection process.
- It helps parents to see that their children are getting the best learning opportunities.

Signs that planning is getting out of hand

- You spend longer planning than you do actually working with children.
- You are writing things out that everyone knows and no one reads.
- You can't remember what on earth you meant when you wrote it down.
- Planning folders take up more space than the toys.
- You have to drink alcohol to face doing it!

Ways of speeding up your planning

- Do your planning on the computer and always make a back-up copy.
- Learn how to use the 'cut and paste' function.
- Learn how to use the 'save as' function so that you can adapt your notes.
- Use symbols where possible, and number curriculum outcomes.

○ Get helpers, students and assistants to contribute towards the planning.
○ Work out what is really necessary – and stick to it!

Different types of planning

There are lots of different types of plans that need to be completed.

○ Activity plans – relate to an individual activity, a bit like a recipe card! These are useful if someone else is to carry out an activity that you have planned. Students often need to produce these as part of their coursework. Some settings develop a bank of these plans.

○ Daily and weekly plans – show the 'batting order' of the day or week and contain details. They are probably the most useful plans of all. Make sure that you jot things onto these plans that you are likely otherwise to forget! Staffing, curriculum objectives and the needs of individual children can all be put on these plans.

○ Medium-term plans – sometimes called curriculum plans or outline plans. They are used to show what activities are likely to be carried out and how they link to the curriculum. Plans may last a month, six weeks or sometimes a term.

○ Long-term plans – give an outline of what is to be achieved over a period of time. In nurseries this might be over a term or even a year.

○ Individual plans – needed for babies and often toddlers. They show activities, equipment and the role of the adult for each child.

○ Individual education plans (see List 65 Drawing upon individual education plan) – used when particular areas of a child's development need to be focused on in a structured way or when a child's needs are different to those of their group.

LIST 25   Using themes

Planning using specific themes can provide a focus for activities with children.

○ Go for themes that are open-ended and flexible enough to work in many different ways and across the curriculum.
○ Look for themes that will help children make connections between what they have already experienced and new knowledge.
○ Avoid abstract concepts as themes. Young children may not get the connection between hot and cold and black and white!
○ Think hard and long about whether the theme is relevant, e.g. do babies really care about cars!
○ Avoid planning a theme just to impress parents.
○ Think hard about your knowledge base. If you know nothing about China, there is a real danger that you will just be giving the children a stereotypical and superficial view.
○ Don't worry if your theme does not cover the entire curriculum. Pick out those activities that will work well. This avoids situations when children only have yellow paint or have to pretend to be elephants while riding a tricycle.
○ Change your plans if the children are obviously bored and uninterested!

Themes that work well include:

○ boxes
○ shopping
○ growing up
○ my family
○ holiday
○ food
○ homes
○ features in the local environment, such as canals, farms, the seaside, motorways.

Ideas for Activities | 4

LIST 26 — Failsafe activities for mathematics

Sand, water and dough are great for teaching mathematics (see Lists 15, 16 and 17).

Measuring length

○ Cut up straws into different lengths.
○ Stick them into the sand tray so that they are poking up.
○ Children pick out three and see which one is the longest.

Recognizing numbers

○ Use a dice with numerals (you can adapt a traditional dice by putting stickers over the dots).
○ Each child has a beaker and a spoon. They roll the dice to determine how many spoonfuls of sand to put in the beaker.
○ The first to fill up their beaker makes a sandcastle and wins!

Number bonds

○ Spread fairy cake papercases out on a tray.
○ Each child rolls the dice and makes out of dough the number of cakes shown on the dice.
○ Draw children's attention to the number of cakes that have been made and the number of cases still to be filled.

Subtraction

○ Use a small cup or beaker to make sandcastles.
○ Children roll the dice to determine how many they can squash flat.

One-to-one matching

○ Put some floating boats in the water tray (you can also use large leaves).
○ Ask the children if they can put a toy animal or other object onto each one.

LIST 27

Developing speaking and listening abilities

Developing children's language in the early years is essential. While some children never seem to stop chatting, others need a little more coaxing.

○ Telling teddy – have a teddy that is always bringing things in for children to look at. The children can listen to the story behind the object.

○ Helping teddy – have a teddy that always has a problem or two. For example, sometimes teddy has problems packing his suitcase and needs a child to tell him what to take on holiday.

○ Sorting activities – put out a tray of objects that lend themselves to being sorted. Button boxes are ideal for this. Make sure that there are things to catch children's interest and chat to them about which ones they like best.

○ Books – reading stories to individual children can be a good way of getting them to chat, as well as listen.

○ Story tapes – some children are happy to curl up and listen to a good story tape, especially if it is one that they know. Try and find the accompanying picture book as well.

○ Games – don't forget those simple games such as 'Simon Says' or 'I-Spy'. They are traditional games because they are so popular!

Encouraging pre-reading skills

Activities for name recognition

Helping children to recognize their name is a good starting point for developing pre-reading skills. They learn that print can carry meaning.

❍ Outdoor treasure hunt for children's names – choose small groups of children at a time to go hunting for their names.
❍ Posting names – as children arrive, they find their name and post it into a box. They can also find and tick their name in the register.
❍ Names in the sand tray – laminate children's names and then hide them in the sand tray.
❍ Picture lotto – use only pictures at first, but then add in their names as well. Eventually make the game into 'Friend lotto'.

Other activities to help pre-reading skills

❍ Jigsaw puzzles.
❍ Matching games and pairs – gradually these can move from pictures to words.
❍ Memory games – children are shown a tray of objects and then have to remember an item that is no longer there.
❍ Nursery rhymes – especially traditional ones with a strong beat and sound pattern. See if children can begin to fill in the missing words if you suddenly stop!

Finally, children need access to simple picture books that become favourites. Make sure that children see adults pointing to the words as they read. Notice when children seem to know the words by heart and correct the adults if they make a 'mistake'.

LIST 29

Making writing fun

Mark-making is the starting point for writing in the early years. Children's writing follows a developmental pattern and is linked to their reading.

Do:

○ Make sure that children see adults writing – set up tables where adults are busy writing and children can join them.
○ Provide opportunities for large-scale mark-making – young children must master their gross motor movements. Use chalk, whiteboards and large-scale painting walls.

Don't:

○ Focus on handwriting skills – writing is actually about words.
○ Make children trace or copy – they don't like it and in the long term it reduces their confidence. They learn that they cannot write unless an adult has helped them.

Ways to encourage writing

○ Have a postbox so that children can write notes to their friends.
○ Provide items from the real writing world, such as passport application forms, junk mail, lottery slips.
○ Write back to children – this is a sure way of encouraging children to keep writing.
○ Use the freepost envelopes that come with the junk mail. They can pretend to post their letters on the way home!

LIST 30   Easy ICT for 3–5s

ICT in the early years is about getting children used to technology. This can include computers as well as other machines and gadgets.

○ Gadgets – children need to learn that technology is about using machines. Look out for these gadgets:
  - key finders
  - torches (with batteries)
  - digital clocks and alarms
  - birthday cards that play a tune when opened.
○ Programmable toys – use programmable toys as an alternative to computers. The advantage is that young children can learn that through their thoughts and actions, they can control something. Roamers, turtles and pixies as well as remote controlled cars can help children see technology in action.
○ Role-play area – make sure that your role-play area reflects the technology that children see in the real world. Look out for toys or redundant objects, such as:
  - digital phone
  - microwave
  - mobile phone
  - laptop or PC
  - cash register with a swipe card for credit cards.
○ Using computers – when children use a computer:
  - be selective about the software that you choose. Avoid software that is really a worksheet in disguise.
  - encourage them to work in pairs so that they can interact with each other.
  - help them to learn about writing, and think about buying a software package that can scribe for children.

LIST 31 Activities for outdoors

The outdoor world is full of learning possibilities. Children are often able to organize their own play and sustain it outdoors. Aim to provide an outdoor classroom!

Treasure hunts

○ Hide a variety of objects outdoors for children to find – think about things such as their names, magnetic numbers and even letters.
○ Encourage children to hide things for others to find as well.

Themed boxes

Provide a series of boxes that have materials and equipment in them ready for children to play with:

○ Wind kit – chime bars, streamers and ribbons, windmills, kites.
○ Rain kit – measuring jugs, paper of different absorbencies, sponges, drainpipes.
○ Sun kit – sunglasses, sheets of fabric.
○ Digging and planting box – seeds, trowels, watering cans, plant pots.
○ Bug hunt box – magnifying sheets, binoculars.

Den-making

○ Provide sheets of plastic and fabric, as well as cups, saucers and those home comforts that children need. Think about using good old cardboard boxes as well.

Gardening

Children love digging and planting things.

○ Work out how much sun your area gets and look out for some basic bulbs, shrubs and bedding plants that will grow.
○ Prepare the soil properly with the children, using compost if needed.
○ Organise a watering rota and enjoy the results.
○ Look out for hyacinths, snowdrops, daffodils, but also vegetables such as potatoes, carrots and peas.

o Always wash hands after touching soil!

Role-play

Children often combine physical play with role-play.

o Put out shopping bags and suitcases, as well as the traditional cups and saucers, for children to use.
o Think about picnic blankets and tents too!
o Finally, don't forget small-world toys such as farm animals, play people and cars.

L I S T 32

Getting creative

Children are naturally creative, interested and keen to explore. Be a good role model and get involved yourself – paint, draw and make things so that children see what fun they can have.

Music

- ○ Don't lock up the musical instruments – the more available they are, the more the children will use them and develop their skills. If you really can't stand the noise, put the instruments in groups so that they make similar sounds, e.g. all the shakers together.
- ○ Play games where children have to shake, rattle or clap to a beat – find songs that have a strong beat to them.
- ○ Play hot and cold games. One child has to find a hidden object, the others make sounds that are either loud if the child is getting close, or quiet if they are moving away.
- ○ Look out for songs that use the children's names.

Painting

- ○ Use trays of paint with the primary colours on them – this avoids washing up pots of paint and also helps children learn to mix colours.
- ○ Use brushes of different sizes, especially large ones.
- ○ Give children opportunities to paint on a large scale and also to paint together.

Modelling

- ○ Look out for good quality junk! Children enjoy using things that are a bit different, that sparkle or have some tactile properties.
- ○ Make sure that glue really does stick and scissors do cut! Provide staplers, masking tape and proper scissors.
- ○ Don't focus on what the model is meant to be. Young children often feel pressurised into making 'something' when quite often they are happy simply exploring and being creative.

Favourite books

It is always worth having to hand some books that you know will grab children's attention. It means that you can count on them during a wet playtime or when you have few minutes to spare. Look out for some of these:

- *Alfie and the Birthday Surprise* by Shirley Hughes
- *Avocado Baby* by John Burningham
- *Can't You Sleep, Little Bear?* by Martin Waddell
- *Come Away from the Water, Shirley* by John Burningham
- *Dear Zoo* by Rod Campbell
- *Elmer* by David McKee
- *I Want My Potty* by Tony Ross
- *Rosie's Walk* by Pat Hutchins
- *Six Dinner Sid* by Inga Moore
- *The Great Big Enormous Turnip* by Helen Oxenbury
- *The Owl Who Was Afraid of the Dark* by Jill Tomlinson
- *The Tiger Who Came to Tea* by Judith Kerr
- *The Wild Washerwomen* by John Yeoman
- *We're Going on a Bear Hunt* by Michael Rosen
- *Where's Spot?* by Eric Hill.

Favourite nursery rhymes

A good nursery rhyme book is a fantastic investment. They help teach children to discriminate between sounds, which is an essential skill when learning to read.

Aim to teach children a repertoire of nursery rhymes while they are with you.

Classic counting rhymes

○ *Ten Green Bottles*
○ *There Were Ten in the Bed*
○ *Five Fat Sausages Sizzling in the Pan*
○ *Five Little Ducks Went A-swimming One Day*
○ *Five Little Speckled Frogs*
○ *Five Currant Buns in a Baker's Shop*
○ *Two Little Dicky Birds Sat on a Wall.*

Traditional rhymes

○ *Bye Baby Bunting*
○ *Tom, Tom the Piper's Son*
○ *Hickory, Dickory, Dock*
○ *Sing a Song of Sixpence*
○ *Ring-a-Ring o' Roses*
○ *Wee Willie Winkie*
○ *Hey Diddle Diddle.*

Working with Children | 5

LIST 35 Settling in children

It is worth giving priority to settling in new children. Anxious children are likely to generate anxious parents.

- ○ Get background information about a child's previous experience of being left. If a child has only ever experienced being with a family member or has had an unhappy experience, the process will take longer.
- ○ Never let a parent 'do a runner'. It only stores up problems for the future as the child learns to cling more to prevent the parent from going off.
- ○ Think about what children learn during a visit. Some children learn that they like school or nursery because it is a place where mummy or daddy plays with them. They then get a nasty shock when their parent leaves!
- ○ Make sure that children have got to know one member of staff well before being left. This can be done through a series of three or four quite short visits where the member of staff takes a particular interest in the child. During these visits:
    - use a puppet or bring out a toy that will intrigue or tempt the child
    - encourage parents to take a bit of a back seat so that the child learns to play with the keyworker
    - test the strength of the keyworker's relationship with the child by arranging for the parents to pop out of sight for a minute
    - gradually build up the length of time that the parents are out of sight.

LIST 36   Tips for filling spare moments

Times when children are not engaged in play or are waiting for something to happen can be a problem. These are the moments when they are likely to get themselves into trouble. So look out for ways of avoiding this (see also List 8 Getting a good routine).

○ Think carefully about your routine.
○ Stagger times when children need to be on the move to avoid crowd control problems.
○ Sing songs and do action rhymes if children have to wait for any reason.
○ Give children something to fiddle with rather than wait for them to find something.
○ See children as potential helpers and give them a small task to do.
○ Make sure that you put enough activities or toys out.
○ Change or vary the activities when children are beginning to lose interest.
○ Chat to children so that they have some adult attention that is positive.
○ Carry a puppet on you which you can pop out.
○ Keep a notepad and pencil with you and whip it out so that children can do a spot of drawing.
○ Draw a smiley face on a child's index finger and do the same on yours. Now they can meet up and have a little chat.

LIST 37   Praise and rewards

Everyone likes to be valued and recognized. Children are no different, and praising and rewarding them can make a huge difference to their behaviour.

○ Attention – the best way of valuing children is to give them plenty of attention. Talk to them and take an interest in what they are doing. Remember to ask them whether they are pleased with themselves and how they are feeling. Don't let children learn to 'steal' your attention, e.g. by tapping you on the back.

○ Praise – this is the easiest and cheapest option with young children. It is also very effective. A simple 'you have been playing well' or 'well done, you are walking' works a treat. Praise works best when:
  – it is sincere and given generously
  – it is given frequently
  – it comes while children are showing the wanted behaviour
  – we tell children exactly why they are being praised.

○ Stickers – children love these, but give them out fairly so that they know how to get them, and avoid situations where children learn that stickers are only given to the naughty ones. If you use white office stickers you can write the child's name on them and the reason why they have got one.

○ Certificates – these are better with older children, but be aware that parents can get very competitive about them.

○ Food, including sweets – in these days of child obesity, this is not really an option.

LIST 38   Bites, smacks and grabs!

When it comes to lashing out, most young children will have their moments, but aggressive behaviour of any type needs to be managed effectively.

○ Avoid direct eye contact with the aggressor – some children learn that aggressive behaviours guarantee adult attention.

○ Soothe the victim and avoid giving attention immediately to the aggressor.

○ Know that one bite generally leads to another. Once a child has bitten another, extra vigilance is required to prevent another bite. Once the victim has been dealt with, keep the attacker very busy.

○ Do not isolate aggressive children, but coach them alongside other children.

○ Avoid situations where the child learns that if they bite or are aggressive, they will get an adult all to themselves!

○ Keep an incident book – think about what prompted the behaviour.

○ Consider whether there are enough sensory and challenging activities available – some bites and aggressive behaviours are a result of frustration and boredom.

○ Feeling tired and hungry is a lethal combination – get food and drink into children and make sure that they do not become over-excited when tired.

○ Give opportunities for children to play by themselves and to have their own spaces, toys and territory – sharing all the time can be hard work.

○ Avoid reminding the child of their behaviour – this can teach children how to get adult attention.

Preventing tantrums

Many children from around 18 months onwards will have a tantrum at some time or another. They are linked to children's frustration and difficulties in communication. Tantrums are unpleasant for everyone, so the best strategy is to avoid them in the first place.

- Think ahead. Remove temptation, especially when children are too young for explanation.
- Make sure that children do not get overtired, hot or hungry.
- Give children enough advance warning of what is happening next.
- Avoid giving something to young children that has to be taken away from them.
- Use distraction wherever possible.
- Avoid rushing children.

LIST 40 Dealing with tantrums

There are different strategies to deal with tantrums, but the tips below are worth considering.

- Do not fuel the tantrum with your own anger.
- Stay near the child and acknowledge their anger.
- Keep calm and consider moving the child to somewhere quieter.
- Have one go at reasoning, distracting or bribing and then stop.
- Do not appear to be distressed by the tantrum.
- When the tantrum is finished, make no comment about the behaviour, but be ready to physically reassure.

When tantrums have become a habit:

- Think hard about the underlying cause of the habit.
- Do not get angry with the child.
- If safe, simply remove yourself and pretend not to notice.
- Avoid direct eye contact.
- Do not make an issue of it afterwards.
- Praise the child as soon as they begin to do something else.
- Give children enormous amounts of praise and positive attention so that they do not need to use temper tantrums as a way of getting adult attention.

Using puppets

LIST 41

Puppets are a great way to get children's attention and also to have fun. Use them to encourage wanted behaviour and also to distract young children.

Choosing a puppet

○ Make sure that you really 'bond' with any puppet that you are buying – you may find that you prefer an animal to a doll or vice versa.

○ Choose a puppet with a moveable mouth.

○ Remember that small puppets can be more versatile than the type that sits on your lap.

○ Make sure that your puppet fits your hand snugly.

○ Visit www.puppetsbypost.com to view a wide selection of puppets.

Keeping the magic of a puppet

○ Make sure that your puppet is brought out 'alive'. Don't let children see you put it on your hand.

○ Do not leave your puppet lying around when you are not using it.

○ Keep it special. Do not let children use it, but do encourage them to touch or stroke it.

○ Make eye contact with your puppet to bring it to life.

○ Make smooth rather than sudden jerky movements.

○ If your puppet is an animal, stroke it as you talk to the children.

Helping children to concentrate

There are some basic conditions that we can create to help children concentrate. Too often adults ignore these and then moan that children don't settle down to anything.

○ Make sure that the room is well ventilated – 18ºC is an ideal temperature.

○ Provide food and drinks – it is harder to concentrate when you are dehydrated or hungry.

○ Let children use the toilet! A full bladder impedes concentration.

○ Go for bursts of physical activity, especially on wet days when children have not been outside.

○ Provide sensory activities – sand, water and dough are all winners.

○ Avoid activities where children are sitting down and listening for long periods.

○ Make sure that activities are genuinely interesting for children.

○ Think about the surprise element – what is new for them to play with or do today?

○ Praise, or even give a sticker, to those children who have been able to play and concentrate.

○ Make sure that your routine does not mean that children are frequently interrupted in their play – this teaches them that there is no point in getting going.

○ Finally, don't fall into the trap of thinking that concentration is about quietness. Concentration is about sustaining attention on the same activity. This means that if your children play noisily for an hour together they are actually concentrating.

LIST 43 Building confidence and independence

Children who can do things for themselves are more likely to develop self-esteem.

Activities to promote independence

- ○ Tidying up.
- ○ Getting dressed – putting on coats, shoes, etc.
- ○ Pouring drinks.
- ○ Making simple snacks – cutting up fruit and vegetables.
- ○ Choosing materials and activities.
- ○ Wiping and drying tables.
- ○ Washing up paint brushes.

Some tips

- ○ Do not worry if children struggle a little from time to time. Providing they are not giving up, and are still keen to keep going, this can be excellent learning.
- ○ Praise children when they persevere.
- ○ Give children enough time – rushing them or stepping in to help too often can teach them that they are not competent.
- ○ When children become frustrated, explain that with practice they will improve. Let them know that all children have moments when they cannot do something straight away and that this is normal.
- ○ Make sure that children feel that they are valued for who they are, not what they can achieve.

Listening to children

Developing children's speech means spending time encouraging them to talk to us. While some children seem born to talk, others are more reluctant and will need us to be good listeners.

○ Give children time – young children often need a moment to have a think and formulate their ideas.

○ Get settled yourself – children often sense when adults are about to rush off and so decide that there is no point in saying much.

○ Avoid interrogating children, especially asking stupid questions such as 'what colour is this?' or 'is this the largest?' They know that you know the answer already.

○ Follow the child's pace and topics of interest – does it matter if they only want to talk about dinosaurs?

○ Avoid interrupting or second-guessing what a child is about to say.

○ Don't correct children's speech or pronunciation overtly. Instead, re-use the same sentence structure or word when you talk, but 'recast' it back correctly.

○ Acknowledge what they've said and make interested comments that show you have been listening.

○ Make sure that you know what to do if a child tells you something that gives concern. Be aware of the child protection procedures where you work.

Coping with Christmas

Christmas is one of those times of year that can be draining rather than fun.

- Don't start Christmas in October – get it over with in just a couple of weeks.
- Avoid hyping Christmas – not all children will celebrate it.
- Keep a good routine going – children react badly to day after day of mayhem.
- Keep any play or nativity simple – parents just want to see their children dressed up.

Cards, decorations and presents

- Try to incorporate the making of Christmas cards, calendars and decorations into the usual planning. Go for creativity rather than cloning.
- Make a simple calendar by taking a photograph of a child and sticking on a calendar tab.
- Make simple cards by giving children collage materials that reflect Christmas, such as tinsel, glitter and sequins. See what they can come up with by themselves.
- Get out the clay so that children can give parents an interesting ornament!

The Christmas party

- Don't expect children to like Father Christmas – he is a stranger and who wants to sit on a stranger's lap anyway?
- If you put out the cakes and biscuits, don't expect children to eat the sandwiches.
- Think of simple games and play them in the weeks beforehand – try Hunt the Thimble, Musical Statues and Okey Cokey.

Observation and Assessment 6

Reasons for observing children

Babies and children are fascinating. Stand back and watch what they can do and how they think!

○ Parents need reassurance and will want to know what their children are doing. While digital photos and snapshot observations are great for this, make sure that you know what your policy is and that you have obtained parental consent first.
○ Children play for longer and are more contented if you put out the right toys, activities and equipment. If you have observed children's interests, you are more likely to hit the right buttons.
○ You can work out what is affecting children's behaviour. If you observe a child, you might be able to work out what is triggering poor behaviour. Observe, too, the reactions of adults when a child does misbehave. Maybe the adults are unwittingly fuelling the problem!
○ Watching children also means that you can think about the progress that they are making. Sometimes we do not realise just how well a child is doing or how they have changed until we have focused on them.
○ You may be able to work out why a child is not responding or progressing in the way you might expect. Quite often you will have a 'hunch' from unconscious observation. By observing the child you might realise the basis for the hunch, e.g. the child is not fully hearing. Getting early help for children can really make a difference.

A quick tour of observation methods

Observation is increasingly becoming central to planning. Use a variety of methods to build up a picture of children.

Checklists and tick charts

These are:

o quick and easy to use
o good for monitoring skills and progress against developmental milestones.

But:

o there is a danger of producing pages of ticks that are not read by others
o they do not provide information about the child's interests and disposition
o watch out for poorly written assessment statements.

Written notes or snapshots

These are:

o great for jotting down what children are doing and are interested in
o helpful for capturing spontaneous behaviours
o useful for sharing with parents.

But:

o hard to record for any length of time.

Audio recordings

Use MP3 players, dictaphones and tape recorders to catch children's speech and language. These are:

o helpful when monitoring children's progress in speech
o wonderful to pass on to parents.

Videos and photographs

These are:

○ a good way of capturing what children are doing or have produced
○ good for sharing with parents and children
○ easy to use.

But:

○ remember to seek parents' permission and check that they are happy for images to be displayed.

Time samples

Children are observed at five or ten minute intervals. This is:

○ good for seeing what groups and individual children do over a session
○ useful to share with parents.

But:

○ it is easy to become distracted and forget to record in the allotted slot.

Target child

This involves minute-by-minute observation of an individual child. The observer uses a coded format.

This is:

○ good for focusing on particular skills.

But:

○ practice is required in order to be quick at using the codes
○ it can be labour intensive.

How and what to observe

Here are a few practical tips about how to observe children.

Keeping out of the way

- Avoid eye contact with children.
- Look for a vantage point where you are partially obscured.
- Try to look as if you are doing something else.
- If children come over and are interested, sound bored and do not make eye contact!
- Use the zoom on videos and cameras.

Assessing children directly

- Try and avoid making children feel that they are being tested.
- Create situations where observations are part of play.
- Think about the timing of the assessment – is the child hungry or tired?

When you are observing there are several things you need to look at.

Physical appearance

- Does the child seem in good health?

Physical movements

- Are movements co-ordinated?
- How relaxed is the child?
- Is hand preference clear?

Speech

- How much language is the child using?
- Are vocalisations expressive and clear?

Social attachments

- Is the child interested in other children?
- Does the child have particular friendships?
- Does the child look for the support and attention of adults?

Concentration

○ Is the child able to settle into play or concentrate on an activity?
○ Does the child seem aware of their surroundings?

LIST 49 Know your milestones

- ○ Refer to developmental milestones to help you make accurate assessments.
- ○ Use either of these books for quick reference:
  - − *From Birth to Five Years* by Mary Sheridan (Routledge)
  - − *Child Development: An Illustrated Guide* by Carolyn Meggitt (Heinemann).
- ○ Try this quiz:

True or false?
1 Most children at 15 months have two to six recognisable words
2 Most two-year-olds can pedal a tricycle
3 Most four-year-olds can eat skilfully with a spoon and fork
4 Most three-year-olds can count to rote to twenty or more
5 Most two-year-olds have 200 or more words
6 Most three-year-olds can cut with toy scissors
7 Most four-year-olds know several nursery rhymes correctly
8 Most five-year-olds can match ten colours
9 Most babies at three months can sit up unsupported
10 Most babies at nine months understand 'no'.

Answers
1 T, 2 F, 3 T, 4 F, 5 F, 6 T, 7 T, 8 T, 9 F, 10 T

Sharing information with parents

Observations should be shared with parents. It helps parents to learn more about their child and what we do with them when they are with us.

○ Make sure that parents understand that their child will be routinely observed. Get written consent.

○ Talk to parents about the methods that are used and how the information is recorded and stored.

○ Check that they are happy for photographs and videos to be used.

Talking to parents about observations

○ Avoid storing up problems. Routinely talk to parents when you have done an observation – even if this is just in passing.

○ Avoid using comparative language, such as he is one of our brighter ones, as this can fuel inter-parental rivalry – some parents will always boast to others!

○ Encourage parents to look out for milestones or skills at home.

○ Ask parents if there is anything their child does that they would like you to report back on or photograph.

Sharing concerns

○ Avoid alarming parents, but simply explain what you have observed or expected to observe.

○ Ask them if your observation matches their thoughts and experiences.

○ Suggest that further observations might be necessary and/or provide ideas of what the parents might be able to do, such as arrange a hearing test or visit a doctor.

○ Try also to collect information that will be positive for parents to hear and share this immediately with them.

Writing records

LIST 51

Keeping records is an important part of working with children. It can be a bit of a minefield though, so here are a few pointers:

○ Aim to write records in a positive way – labelling children negatively in their earliest years is unfair.

○ Avoid the horrible global terms of 'less able' or 'more able' – they may come back to haunt you one day. Remember that Einstein's teachers rated him as bright but not outstanding!

○ Think carefully about how assessments might affect a child's future – when in doubt, be on the child's side!

○ Remember that parents have access to records – be sensitive, their child is precious.

○ When writing concerns about children, always back up your statement with some concrete evidence that provides explanation for your conclusion.

○ Collect photos, art work and writing to supplement children's records. Annotate them with post-it notes.

○ Keep records up to date. Inspectors will want to see how your record-keeping system works.

○ If you have many records to keep, make a list each week of certain children to focus on.

LIST 52 Tips to make record-keeping easier

Record-keeping can be time consuming, but try out a few of these tips:

○ Look critically at what you do
○ Decide what really needs to be recorded about children's progress.
○ Go for the minimum wherever possible – one piece of a child's work or a photograph might provide information about several developmental areas or curriculum outcomes.
○ Think about the best way of collecting and storing information.
○ Avoid pages of endless checklists. Let's be honest – who really does read them later on?
○ Look at the format of record sheets – think about whether they really work.
○ Be bold and consider adapting or designing your own.
○ Think about whether you can put some records onto computer – this can be faster, especially where you are writing similar things for each child.
○ Make a regular time slot each week when you focus on record-keeping.
○ Try having a rota system so that you update a few children's records at a time.
○ Keep a notebook so that on a day-to-day basis you can jot odd things down that you have noticed about children.

Parents

LIST 53   Reasons to work with parents

Once upon a time, parents were outsiders when it came to the
education and even care of their own children! Today, it is essential
to work with parents effectively. There are good reasons why you
should always look for ways of working with parents.

- Children settle in more quickly.
- Parents are less anxious.
- You can find out pieces of information that will make working
  with children easier.
- Conversations about children's behaviour become easier to
  manage.
- Parents are more likely to forgive you if you get an aspect of their
  child's care wrong.
- Parents will recommend your setting to other parents.
- Parents are more likely to help out, maybe as helpers or even
  supporting the odd bring and buy sale.
- The relationship between staff and parents is considered during
  the inspection process.

LIST 54 Understanding the pressures on parents

It's easy to forget that parents can be under huge amounts of pressure. This in turn can affect how they react to us. Maybe those small niggles and complaints are really symptoms of something else!

○ Financial difficulties – many parents might not want to leave their children to go back to work.
○ Guilt – some parents feel guilty that they are leaving their children to go back to work.
○ Relationships – some parents may be going through a rough patch with their partners.
○ Tiredness – coping with children, working and day-to-day living puts huge pressures on parents.
○ Media – there is an image that parents should be happy and enjoying their children at all times. Mothers are meant to be radiant, patient and simply perfect. That can be a bit hard to live up to!
○ Competitiveness – some people are determined to make parenthood into an Olympic sport. This can make other parents feel inadequate.

Showing new parents around

Parents have increasing choice about where they should send their children. This means that it is essential to 'sell' your setting.

○ Think about the strengths of your setting and make sure that these are shown or explained to parents.

○ Choose times when children are likely to be happily playing.

○ Avoid the start and end of sessions, as well as lunchtimes, when it tends to be more chaotic.

○ Make sure that everyone in the setting knows the date and time of the visit.

○ Check that the entrance looks inviting.

○ Decide who will be the child's likely keyworker and make sure that this person is available to talk to parents and spend time with the child.

○ Make sure that parents have enough time to get a good feel for your setting.

○ Encourage them to ask questions.

○ Take time to explain to parents why you work in the way you do and your philosophy, especially when it comes to:
  – keyworkers
  – settling in
  – the level of structured activities and play
  – your approach towards children's behaviour
  – fees, opening hours and provision of nappies (if appropriate)
  – policy on helping children learn to read, count, etc. (if appropriate).

○ Give parents a prospectus and invite them to visit again if they wish.

LIST 56 Home visits

Home visits before a child starts can be a fantastic way to get to know parents. It can make settling in a lot easier for everyone!

Why home visits are popular

○ It is easier to get to know parents when they are relaxed and on home ground.
○ They allow parents to mention things that they are embarrassed about others hearing.
○ Children feel that they can trust you as they have seen you at their home.
○ We can learn more about children and their needs.

Making home visits work

○ Look and act relaxed – don't wear formal clothes, such as a suit.
○ Let parents know that the purpose of the visit is to help with settling in.
○ Give them a mobile number in case they need to cancel your visit.
○ Check with parents the day before that they are expecting you.
○ Take along some toys so that you can play with the child.
○ Ask the child to show you their favourite toys, videos or photographs.
○ Find out from parents what their child enjoys doing and who they like to play with.
○ Talk to parents about what their child will be doing when they start.
○ Encourage parents to ask questions.

Safety

○ Always make sure that you have left a record of the address of where you are going for colleagues and what time you should be back.
○ Take a mobile with you and leave it on.
○ Consider whether you should visit in pairs.

Settling in parents

It can be hard for parents when their child first starts school or nursery. So, let's make it easier for them.

○ Take time to give parents information. They will need to know:
  - what time to bring their child
  - what their child should bring with them
  - how long their child will be staying
  - what to do if their child cannot come
  - what will happen when they first arrive
  - who will be responsible for looking after their child
  - how you will let them know if there is a problem.

○ Make sure that parents know what they should do when it's time to leave their child. This is always easier if the child has got to know their keyworker and if they have visited the setting before. Avoid situations where children are 'tugged' away from their parent. This is a recipe for distress!

○ Encourage parents to meet and talk to each other – new parents can find great comfort by getting to know each other.

○ Take time at the end of the first session to provide feedback to parents about what their child has done – be honest, but also positive!

LIST 58 Keeping in contact with parents

Many parents find it hard to pop in and spend time in the setting. So here are some ways in which we can keep in contact.

○ Meeting and greeting – a quick word now and then can really help when parents drop off their child. Try and prioritise this as a time for parents.

○ Home slips – these are great for jotting down information each day, are liked by parents and really needed if you are caring for babies and toddlers.

○ Home books – these can be used as a two-way notepad. Parents can jot down snippets about what their child has been doing at weekends or any problems that they are having. You could stick in the odd photograph so that parents can 'see' their child.

○ Webcams – these are really controversial, but some parents like being able to see their child at any point.

○ Reports – some places do weekly reports, but this can be hard if you are working with large numbers of children. It can be hard to write about any concerns.

○ Newsletters – great for keeping groups of parents up to speed about what you are doing.

○ Letters – be careful that you get the tone of the letter right. If it's too formal parents may feel that you are unapproachable.

LIST 59 Information evenings and open days

Parents like to know how their child is getting along, so information evenings and open days are essential. These times can be used as a way of introducing parents to each other too.

Open days

○ Look out for activities that children will really enjoy.
○ Avoid activities that require significant staff involvement, otherwise no one will be available to talk to parents.
○ Expect that children will be distracted and want to see their parents.
○ Use open days as a chance to explain to parents what their children are getting out of the session.

Evenings

○ Make sure that everywhere looks tidy and attractive.
○ Put plenty of children's work out.
○ Use this as an opportunity to put out useful information.
○ Put some background music on, otherwise it will seem very quiet.
○ Possibly show a video of the children at play.
○ Look at your room layout and ensure that parents can talk to you without being overheard.
○ Consider drinks and nibbles – they can make everyone more relaxed!

Talking to parents

○ Smile!
○ Make sure that you have things to show parents and any records available.
○ Ask parents how they feel their child is doing.
○ Avoid comparing children – parents tend to know each other and word gets around fast.
○ Keep a jotter with you so that you do not forget things that parents tell you.

It is unlikely that you will please all the parents, all the time, however hard you try!

How many of these do you recognize?

○ My child hasn't got any friends.
○ No one noticed that my child was sopping wet.
○ My child's clothes are covered in paint/mud/chalk.
○ The new trousers/shoes/top have been ruined.
○ I am worried that my child is not being stretched enough.
○ Someone has taken my child's coat/bag/toy.
○ My child didn't get a turn at...
○ I didn't get the letter about...
○ My child hasn't been chosen for the part of Mary/Joseph/lead donkey.
○ My child is always out late.
○ My child doesn't like...
○ My child has lost their...
○ Are the snacks and drinks organic?

So next time you get collared, smile sweetly, deal with the problem and remember you are not alone!

LIST 61

Encouraging parents to help out

An extra pair of hands can be extremely useful. But are you making the most of your parents?

Ways to recruit parents

○ Put out a general plea in a letter – state the type of tasks for which you need help.
○ Ask a parent directly.
○ Send a personal note home.

First session

○ Think about having an informal induction.
○ Find out what they do, know and are interested in.
○ Match tasks to parents' skills and experience.
○ Take the time to train parents so that they can understand what to do.
○ Talk through your setting's policy on confidentiality.

Other tips

○ Invite keen parents to a training session.
○ Avoid giving parents the boring jobs, such as sharpening pencils or being stuck in the kitchen.
○ Thank them at the end of the session.
○ Give parents some feedback so that they know their work is valued.
○ Be mindful about what you say about children, just in case it gets home.
○ Don't take their work for granted – remember that parents can vote with their feet!

Fundraising and social events

While fundraising events can bring in a bit of cash to buy a few extras, they are also great ways of getting to know parents. Think about doing a few of these!

- Pub quiz
- Charity auction
- Garden party
- Summer fete or fair
- Christmas fete or fair
- Booze-cruise outing
- Karaoke evening
- It's A Knockout event
- Pantomime
- Jumble sale
- Car-boot sale
- Coffee morning
- Trips to zoos, theatres, rock concerts
- Wine tasting
- Clothes parties
- Toys and books sale.

Special Needs and Inclusion

LIST 63   Inclusion – common questions

- *What is inclusion?* Inclusion is an approach to education, but also social policy. Instead of children 'having to fit in' or be excluded attending a special school, the aim is to make changes to the way we work to ensure that we meet the needs of all children.
- *What are special educational needs (SEN)?* This term, along with 'additional needs', is used to describe children who need extra support, equipment or time in order to learn.
- *Do we have to take children with SEN in mainstream?* In 1989 the UK signed up to the United Nation's Convention on the Rights of the Child. One of the articles states that children should not be discriminated against. Another also states that all children have the right to education. Forcing children out of mainstream education on account of a special need would breach the convention. Subsequent legislation has firmly laid out the principle of inclusion.
- *Do I need to be specially trained to work with children with SEN?* No, not unless a child has a significant physical care or medical need.
- *How will I know how to work with the child then?* The key is often to listen carefully to parents, other professionals and, more importantly, learn to observe and get to know the child. You may also have to think carefully about whether your usual way of working with children is appropriate.

Early identification

Early identification of children with special or additional needs is considered to be essential.

○ Observe children frequently – remember to consider normative development charts or milestones to gauge children's progress.

○ Build good relationships with parents – this makes for more effective working and it becomes easier for everyone to share the odd concern.

○ Always question the root cause of a child's unwanted behaviour – throwing a puzzle on the floor might be a result of poor hand–eye coordination caused by a visual impairment.

○ Avoid making assumptions – a child from a refugee family may be unresponsive not through trauma but because of a learning difficulty or hearing impairment.

○ Observe children's physical development carefully – balance, locomotive skills and hand–eye coordination can all be affected by other conditions.

○ Share any thoughts or concerns that you have immediately with parents. Focus on the importance of getting it right for the child and, if necessary, put together a plan to observe and support the child further (see also List 65 on individual education plans).

○ Take up training opportunities, especially those run by professionals such as speech and language therapists. This can help you learn to identify children whose development is atypical.

LIST 65   Drawing up an individual education plan

To support children with special or additional needs you should draw up an individualised programme. Terms used for these plans can vary but in England and Wales they are known as individual education plans or IEPs.

○ *Which children will need a plan?* The aim is that only children who need additional support over and above that which you would provide in any case will have a plan.

○ *Who draws up the plan?* Usually it is the person who acts as a keyworker or main support for the child, in conjunction with parents and the person in the setting who is responsible for SEN. In England and Wales, this is the SENCO.

○ *What do I put in a plan?*
 – Agree with parents three or four targets that are realistic for the child to achieve over a period of around eight weeks.
 – Decide on how the child will be helped to achieve them, e.g. adult support required, type of activities.
 – Write down who will be responsible for making sure that the plan is put into effect and when it will be reviewed.

○ *What happens next?* The plan is reviewed with parents. New targets might be set. Other professionals might be approached if there are still concerns about the child's progress. Sometimes children will not need any further IEPs.

Tips to help children with learning difficulties

The term learning difficulties is a broad one, but it encompasses children who may need a little extra support to retain and process information. The tips below are worth trying out and putting into your everyday practice as they work well with plenty of other children too!

Memory and concentration

- Use visual aids, such as props, pictures and puppets.
- Find ways of using sand, dough and water (see Lists 15, 16 and 17 on these subjects).
- Show rather than tell children what they should be doing.
- Use songs as well as words when giving instructions.
- Get children to repeat instructions.
- Keep information interesting and relevant to the child.

Completing tasks

- Break down tasks into smaller steps, such as identifying a toy that needs to be put away, picking it up, finding where it lives and putting it away.
- Praise and, if necessary, celebrate at the completion of each step.
- Look out for signs of boredom or frustration – always quit while you are ahead!
- Provide reasons and incentives for the child.
- Give children as much independence and choice as possible.

Reinforcement

- Allow and encourage children to repeat the same activity by themselves.
- Change one small element of an activity to challenge the child – instead of finding their name in the sand, the child has to fish it out of a tray using magnetic rods.
- Make sure that children are confident before moving on to other tasks and activities.

Watching out for hearing loss

Hearing loss in young children is more common than you might think. Most hearing loss is temporary and caused by fluid building up in the Eustachian tube. This is sometimes referred to as 'glue ear'. It is essential to identify children who are prone to this type of problem. Does the child:

- ❍ have frequent coughs and colds?
- ❍ have a muffled quality to their speech?
- ❍ appear to withdraw into their own world and become unresponsive?
- ❍ try to stand close to the television or sit close to you at story time?
- ❍ watch a speaker's face intently, especially the mouth?
- ❍ sometimes fail to respond to their name or come when called?
- ❍ sometimes appear to be startled, e.g. the child has been playing and suddenly realises that everyone else is tidying up?

Did you know that...it has been estimated that 80% of children under eight years old will at some time be affected by glue ear.

If you suspect that a child is not fully hearing, you will need to talk to the child's parents. A simple hearing test is then usually arranged via the family doctor.

Working with children who have hearing loss

Here are some tips for working with children who have hearing loss. These tips help other children too, so they are worth using anyway!

- ○ Turn lights on and put as much natural light into the room as possible.
- ○ Turn your face into the light when you speak.
- ○ Check that you have a child's attention before talking.
- ○ Avoid covering your face with your hands – children need to see your mouth.
- ○ Seat children near you during group activities or stories.
- ○ Go up to a child, rather than call to them.
- ○ Identify the subject of a conversation at the start, e.g. 'Cats. Did you see the cats on the wall?'
- ○ Point to the subject of a conversation if possible, e.g. the sand tray, toilets.
- ○ Use props and pictures to help children follow what is happening.
- ○ Speak clearly, but do not shout!
- ○ If a child uses a hearing aid, check that it is working and ask if you can have some spare batteries. Ask parents or even the child to explain how it works.
- ○ Remember to spend time listening to children who have hearing loss too! They will often need some extra time with an adult to help them catch up with their speech and language development.

Identifying and helping children with visual impairment

Being able to see is often taken for granted, and much of our work with children is based round their ability to see things. It's essential, therefore, that we are aware of those children who have some form of visual impairment and may need extra support.

Indicators of visual impairment

Does the child:

- ❍ stand close to the television or stand close by when you are showing things?
- ❍ become frustrated easily by tasks that require hand–eye co-ordination?
- ❍ peer or frown?
- ❍ complain of headaches, frequently rub the eyes or seem tired?
- ❍ have many accidents, such as falls, or have a reputation for being 'clumsy'?
- ❍ ever not appear to notice things that others do, such as a passing airplane?
- ❍ lose concentration easily?

Tips for helping children

- ❍ Find out from parents how they help the child at home.
- ❍ Quietly remind children when they should be wearing glasses.
- ❍ Maximise lighting to avoid shadows and, if necessary, think about table lights where the child plays.
- ❍ Provide resources that are larger, such as large print books or chunky puzzles.
- ❍ Encourage all children to keep passageways clear or chairs and toys out of the way.
- ❍ Make sure that ramps and steps are clearly marked – use fluorescent strips.
- ❍ Make sounds when approaching a child to avoid startling them.

You can also gain further advice from support organisations such as www.look-uk.org, as well as your local sensory impairment team.

LIST 70
Dealing with attention deficit hyperactive disorder (ADHD)

While there is a lot of controversy around ADHD, the reality is that there are many children who find it hard to settle down and concentrate.

○ Remember that all children respond to positive rather than negative environments.

○ Find out what holds the child's interest and make sure that you build on this.

○ Create a calm atmosphere – try soft music and always react calmly to different situations.

○ Praise and acknowledge good behaviour – make sure the child does not learn to use unwanted behaviour to gain your attention.

○ Provide as many multi-sensory opportunities as possible – they really do work!

○ Build some strong routines, but check that they do not leave children waiting around doing nothing.

○ Avoid long explanations – show rather than tell.

○ Plan activities that children can dip in and out of – this is the basis of good play opportunities.

○ Provide plenty of adult support, but keep children active and busy.

○ Provide frequent, positive feedback to the child and consider using stickers.

○ Avoid confrontations – look for ways of making activities into a game.

○ Keep the number of rules down to a minimum but remind children of the boundaries.

Understanding speech and language difficulties

Pronunciation

It is normal for young children to mispronounce many sounds. Pronunciation is dependent on the development of the muscles, jaw and teeth. Generally speaking, children should, however, be intelligible to a stranger at around three years. If this is not the case, it is important that the child's hearing is checked and thereafter they are referred to the speech and language service.

○ Speak clearly. Put in all the sounds of words, e.g. the 't' in water or 'd' in round.
○ Use traditional nursery rhymes as a way of helping children practise the sounds in English.
○ Repeat correctly, and in context, a word that a child has mispronounced – ' I am a mermelade,' 'I think you will make a fantastic mermaid'.

Stammering

Stammering can be a phase that some children go through between the ages of two and four years old because their thoughts do not always match the speed at which they can produce the sounds. It is important that it is sensitively handled so that it remains a phase. Where a child is becoming frustrated, is constantly stammering or has a family history of stammering, they made need a referral to a speech and language therapist.

○ Avoid situations where children have to compete to speak, e.g. 'who can be the first to tell me. . ..'
○ Do not finish off sentences for the child or allow other children to do so.
○ Show the child that you have plenty of time for them so that they do not need to rush to get the words out.
○ Provide opportunities for the child to talk to you without other children being around.
○ Sit down and talk at a slightly slower speed than normal.
○ Do not let other children interrupt you when you are with the child.

Reluctant speakers

Some children do not want to talk. At home they may get their needs met by simply pointing or they may have brothers or sisters who do all the talking for them!

○ Use a puppet for a 'shy' child.

○ Observe to see if the child speaks to others.

○ Avoid giving the child attention for not speaking, but look for situations which might tempt the child to talk, e.g. 'Teddy is in the bag. Let's say hello to him!'

○ Consider using pictures as a starting point for communication. Get the child to pick up a picture of what they want and pass it to you. Acknowledge the request using language. Once the habit is established, hold onto the picture and say what it is. Ask the child to repeat what you have said. Praise.

Support, websites and resources

There is plenty of support around that you can tap into. Don't ever forget the parents though. They are usually experts when it comes to knowing their child and meeting their child's needs!

- Local teams – always begin by contacting your early years team. They will usually be able to give you advice or point you in the right direction for more specialist help. Remember that parental consent is required before children can be seen by specialists.
- Special education advisory team.
- Sensory impairment team.
- Speech and language service.
- Educational psychologist service.
- Social Services (can be useful for funding issues).

Websites

- www.caf.org.uk – a great website which acts a gateway when you are trying to find out more information.
- www.csie.org.uk – provides information on inclusion.
- www.dfes.gov.uk/sen – Department for Education and Skills website giving specific advice and information.

There is a terrific number of voluntary organisations providing support and information for parents and professionals. They are useful for more specific information. Use the Google search engine and have a browse.

Books and resources

- Toy library service – excellent for borrowing specialist toys as well as equipment that will enhance your day-to-day provision.
- *Supporting Special Needs: Understanding Inclusion in the Early Years* by Penny Tassoni (Heinemann).

Staying Safe

LIST 73 — Signs of child abuse

Ensuring safety is a major part of caring for young children. Sadly, some children are victims of abuse. Below is a summary of indicators for neglect and physical and sexual abuse. This is a quick guide and not an exhaustive list. Remember that indicators cannot be taken as conclusive proof.

❍ Make sure that you have read the child protection procedures for your setting. Do you know what you should do if you have concerns about a child? This will usually entail talking to your immediate supervisor, but this does depend on where you work, and remember that child protection procedures do change.

❍ Look out, too, for *What to do if you think a child is being abused.* This is a free publication available from the DfES (ref: 318150). Order it online at www.dfes.gov.uk.

Physical abuse

❍ Injuries in areas not normally associated with everyday bumps and grazes, such on the insides of thighs, the upper arms and neck.

❍ Unusual marks, such as bite marks or bruising patterns, e.g. in the shape of a hand or belt.

❍ Burns or scalds.

❍ Reluctance or hesitation by the child to explain the injury.

Sexual abuse

❍ A surprising amount of sexual knowledge for the child's age, which is revealed during role-play, in drawings or when chatting.

❍ Soiling or wetting in children who are otherwise toilet trained.

❍ Pain on urinating.

❍ Bedwetting.

❍ Bruising and soreness near genital areas.

Neglect

○ Often hungry and tired.

○ Frequent accidents at home, such as scalds, falls and bruises.

○ Unkempt appearance – dirty hair, teeth and clothing.

○ Underweight and general poor health – suffering from constant colds or sores.

Keeping children safe from abusers

Sadly, adults working with children have been known to abuse their positions of trust. This means that it is important to have measures in place to protect them.

Visitors

○ Make sure that entrances are secure, and provide clear signs telling visitors where to go.

○ Check the identification of visitors and provide badges that say who they are.

○ Do not allow visitors to be in situations where they are unsupervised with access to children, even if they are working, e.g. window cleaners or plumbers.

○ Challenge anyone who appears to be 'wandering'. Ask them politely if they are lost or need any help.

Outdoors

○ Check that boundary fences are secure and gates are locked before allowing children out to play.

○ Report to the police any suspicious adults that are hanging around the perimeter of the setting.

○ On trips, do not put children's names on labels, and make sure that adult–child ratios are strictly adhered to.

Volunteers, including parents

○ Make sure that parents and other helpers know that they should not pass on their phone numbers or contact details to children.

○ Make sure that regular volunteers have been officially checked before allowing them unsupervised access to children.

○ Avoid situations when adults (including you) are alone with individual children and out of sight from other adults – leave a door propped open.

Signs of illness in children

Young children can quickly become poorly. Recognizing the early warning signs can be helpful.

Physical signs

- ○ Pale or greyish skin
- ○ Dark rings around the eyes
- ○ Hot to the touch
- ○ Flushed or red cheeks
- ○ Headache
- ○ Vomiting or diarrhoea.

Other signs

- ○ Rubbing eyes
- ○ Fretful and/or tearful
- ○ Comfort behaviours, such as sucking thumbs, rocking or twiddling hair
- ○ Difficulty in concentrating or uninterested in joining in with activities
- ○ Withdrawn behaviour
- ○ Squabbling and over-reacting
- ○ Loss of appetite.

Looking after poorly children

- ○ Take the child away from other children and be reassuring.
- ○ Try to reunite the child with their parents as soon as possible – young children tend not to feign illness!
- ○ Make sure you have a bucket and plenty of tissues near you in case of vomiting.
- ○ Wear disposable gloves if you need to clear up anything messy!
- ○ Remember that you cannot administer any medicine without parental consent.
- ○ Give feverish children plenty of water and, if necessary, take off a layer or two of clothing.

LIST 76 — When to get emergency treatment

Young children's health can go downhill extremely quickly. Occasionally, some children will need emergency treatment.

Seek emergency help if:

○ breathing is rapid, shallow and difficult
○ lips or nails become blue
○ the child has a convulsion or fit
○ the child has a temperature of 38.3C or higher
○ the child complains of a headache that is severe, especially if accompanied by vomiting
○ there is acute and severe pain
○ there are signs of meningitis (see below).

Signs of meningitis

Meningitis develops rapidly and can be a killer. Children need immediate medical attention. It often starts off with flu-like symptoms:

○ fever and drowsiness
○ severe headache
○ dislike of lights and brightness
○ nausea and vomiting
○ stiff neck
○ blotchy skin rash that can look like bruising – test by pressing a glass onto the skin. If the skin does not become pale, seek immediate medical attention
○ babies might arch their backs and also have a high-pitched scream.

Asthma

Children will need access at all times to their inhaler. This is usually blue and is needed when children feel breathless or are having an attack. There are different types of inhalers, so make sure you understand how the one the child uses works. During an attack:

○ keep calm and reassure the child
○ give the inhaler to the child and encourage them to relax

86

o seek emergency help if the inhaler is making no difference and the child's condition is deteriorating.

Epilepsy

There are many different types of seizures, so it is always worth talking to parents about how their child is affected. For tonic-clonic seizures (where a person falls to the ground and loses consciousness):

o remove any dangerous objects
o cushion the head
o do not restrict movement
o put the child in the recovery position
o comfort the child as they gain consciousness
o reassure other children
o allow the child to rest or sleep afterwards
o seek emergency help if this is the first time the child has had a seizure.

For further information visit www.epilepsy.org.uk.

Basic first-aid

It is important to have a good knowledge of first-aid. Children do have accidents! Make sure that you get some training and remember that techniques change and so you will need to keep up to date.

○ Keep calm.
○ Always reassure the child and others around.
○ Get first-aid help if you are not trained.

Bumps, bruises and trapped fingers

○ Put a cold compress (a wet towel or tissues) on the area.
○ Prevent swelling by applying crushed ice wrapped in a towel.

Bumps to the head

○ As above, but keep a close watch on the child.
○ Get help if the child later begins to vomit, has disturbed vision or is drowsy.

Insect stings

○ Try to remove the sting by scraping it out with a fingernail.
○ Do not squeeze the sting!
○ Use a wrapped ice pack to reduce swelling.
○ Get help if the child seems to be showing an allergic reaction, such as serious swelling or difficulty in breathing.

Nosebleed

○ Reassure the child.
○ Keep the head tipped forward.
○ Pinch the soft part of the nose, just under the bridge.
○ Reduce swelling with a cold compress or crushed ice wrapped in a towel.

Grazes

○ Rinse the affected area with cold water.

Preventing cross infection

Germs and children seem to go together! But it is not always inevitable – good approaches to hygiene can significantly reduce the risk of colds and even upset stomachs!

How to prevent airborne attacks!

○ Keep rooms well ventilated – open a window first thing in the morning, whatever the weather.
○ Teach children to cough into their hands (make sure you do this too) and even give stickers for it!
○ Keep snot under control! Carry lots of tissues with you so that children can promptly blow their noses. Make sure that waste tissues get put in a covered bin.
○ Provide plenty of outdoor play opportunities – germs love damp, warm interiors.

How to avoid swallowing the blighters!

○ Wash hands regularly and always before eating or drinking – use soap!
○ Make sure that children wash their hands too, especially after being outdoors and going to the loo.
○ Wear aprons and wash them at a hot temperature.
○ Always use disposable gloves for first-aid and when cleaning up mess.
○ Wash toys and equipment regularly, especially those that are handled a lot, such as bricks.
○ Never be tempted to suck a pencil top or bite your nails!
○ Don't share food – a child's infected hands will also have been touching those crisps!
○ Take a food hygiene course and follow its advice!

How to prevent germs getting under your skin!

○ Cover open cuts or sores with plasters.
○ Rinse any cuts or grazes properly.
○ Dry hands properly, don't just wipe them roughly on your clothes.

L I S T 79 Combating headlice

One of the drawbacks about working with young children is that sometimes they bring their friends along to meet us too! Headlice live on the head and draw blood from the scalp. If you have an itchy scalp and white specks that don't move with a comb, the chances are that you have them! The white specks are the casings from the hatched eggs, while the itchiness is caused by the bites. Headlice seem to favour the back of the head and behind the ears. They are small, brown or translucent, and they don't go away by themselves!

Treatment

- There are many different treatments, but nit combing is always required. Advice should be taken from a chemist.
- Consider getting an electric comb which kills live headlice as it goes!

Avoiding

- Keep your hair tied back.
- Check your own hair regularly and encourage parents to check their children's.
- Make headlice stigma free!
- Avoid putting out hats and scarves for the role-play area.
- Comb your hair like mad!

LIST 80 Dealing with threadworms

While headlice are always in the news, threadworms have remained taboo! But watch out for them because they are very common – statistically one in five children will have a threadworm infestation at any time.

These vile creatures measure about 1cm when fully grown and look like white threads.

The females come out at night and lay their eggs, thus causing an itchy bottom. A cycle then begins where the child scratches their bottom and the eggs are transferred back into their mouths or spread to other people on things the child has been touching.

Treatment

- ○ Tablets are available over the counter at chemists.
- ○ Wash bedding at hot temperatures.
- ○ Encourage parents to put their children in pyjamas at night.

Avoiding

- ○ It's back to basics here! Simply make sure that you and the children wash your hands with hot water and soap before eating and drinking.
- ○ Also make sure that toys that are handled frequently are not put in the mouth and are properly washed.

L I S T 81

Filling out accident books

Accident books are a part of modern life, so make sure you know when and how to fill them in!

Why are they so important?

○ Parents need to know what has happened to their child as some serious problems can have delayed onset, e.g. the symptoms of concussion might not show immediately.

○ It is a registration requirement, and inspectors will check the accident book.

○ It can save you from allegations of physical abuse.

○ You can check whether any particular piece of equipment or area is creating a safety hazard.

When do they need filling in?

○ After any incident, however slight or minor – a bump, scratch or graze.

○ Note that a separate book is usual to record staff accidents.

○ Make sure that you write in the record book immediately.

What's needed?

○ Date and time of accident.

○ Name of child.

○ Circumstances and location of accident.

○ Injuries that occurred.

○ Treatment provided and by whom.

○ Signature – and often that of parent to confirm that they have been advised of the accident.

Your own back care

Everyone working with young children needs to look after their back. A few simple steps can prevent back pain and injury.

○ Pace yourself at the start of the day – this is when your back is at its most vulnerable.

○ Squat rather than bend – this will strengthen your thigh muscles and give you great legs!

○ If you are having a stressful day, spend five minutes at break or lunchtime lying flat on your back.

○ Think carefully about the layout of your room and storage facilities.

○ Make tidying up part of the routine that children are involved in.

○ Do not lift heavy objects, such as furniture or sand trays, by yourself – it is simply not worth it, so ask for help. Under the 1974 Health and Safety Act, your employer has a duty to prevent accidents. This means that if you have notified the management team that there is a problem, they must find a solution. To encourage them to take you seriously, put it in writing and keep a copy.

○ Whenever you can, straighten up completely and walk absolutely tall, with your shoulders back. Make this a habit.

○ If you have been bending over, straighten up and bend slightly the other way to reverse the position.

Coping with Management and Inspection

10

Top tips for managing people

At some point in your working life you are likely to be given responsibility for other staff, whether they are volunteers, parent helpers or other paid staff. Managing other people doesn't have to be difficult, and a bit of tact and diplomacy can go a long way.

○ Lead by example – be enthusiastic, be early and work hard. Don't shirk your duties.
○ Know that problems can always get worse, so deal with them when they arise.
○ Remember that pay is a small factor in why people come to work. More important is the work itself. Make sure that you all work in a dynamic and interesting environment.
○ Look out for those people who have gained in experience, but whose role is still the same. They are likely to become demotivated. Try and give them more responsibility.
○ Recognize other people's hard work:
  – comment on wonderful displays
  – tell parents in front of a staff member or volunteer how good they are
  – write notes when someone has gone the 'extra mile'
  – send in photos and stories about your successes to the local press.
○ Be fair and flexible, not mean – avoid situations where you stick to the rule book so rigidly that you create resentment, e.g. refusing a hardworking member of staff time off to attend the funeral of a friend.

Top ten staff problems

There are a few recurring problems when managing others. You will probably come across some of these!

1 Staff who don't ever seem to arrive on time.
2 Staff who seem to have a constant stream of funerals to go to.
3 Staff who do not notice the time when it is the end of break or lunch.
4 Staff who suddenly notice the time at the end of the day!
5 Staff who have frequent stomach upsets on Mondays and Fridays.
6 Staff who are happy to let others do the work but still get paid.
7 Staff who moan that there is not enough communication but who refuse to come to meetings.
8 Staff who can't read plans.
9 Staff who don't like parents.
10 Staff who don't like children.

Listening and learning

Management is not about telling others what to do. It is more about getting the best from people.

Why take the time to listen?

- ○ People like it – it is linked to feeling valued.
- ○ You are perceived as being approachable.
- ○ It prevents a 'them and us' culture from developing.
- ○ It acts as an early warning system when there are problems.
- ○ It helps you focus on what is really important.
- ○ Small problems and misunderstandings can be sorted out quickly.

Finding the time to listen

It's no good complaining that there is not enough time to talk to the people you are managing. That's a bit like the dairy farmer complaining that there is no time to milk the cows. So, make sure you build your routine around listening to staff members (and parents).

- ○ Get in to work early and do some of your jobs before it gets busy.
- ○ Make cups of tea and coffee at the start and/or end of day and take them around.
- ○ Greet everyone by name when you see them. Remember to ask how they are and be interested in the reply.
- ○ Make sure that the appraisal system is a positive one and keep it up to date.
- ○ If you have an office, keep the door open all times – shut it only when necessary.
- ○ Avoid moaning about how busy/tired/stressed you are. It's usually the same for everyone!

Delegating

Good managers can delegate responsibility to others. This frees up their time and helps them manage more effectively.

Reasons why managers say that they can't delegate

❍ It would be quicker to do it myself.
❍ I am the only one who knows where everything is.
❍ I haven't the time to show anyone else.
❍ I like to do everything myself so that I know that it is done properly.
❍ I like things to be done my way.

Reasons why you should delegate

❍ You were not born doing the things that you do now, you learnt to do them. You also only got quicker because you practised.
❍ By not delegating responsibility, you are denying others the opportunity to learn new skills and gain the experience they may need to be promoted.

How to delegate

❍ Look for whole tasks and areas of responsibility. Do not just delegate the grotty jobs. Usually grotty jobs are part of something more meaningful – cutting up fruit for snack time isn't much fun, but being completely responsible for planning snacks and spending a budget is.
❍ Talk to the person about how they will learn about the role:
  – work out training needs
  – create an action plan
  – agree on how their work will be monitored and supported.
❍ Avoid poking your nose in and meddling – allow people to find their own solutions to mistakes.
❍ Recognize, support and help the person to grow into the role!

Making meetings work

When it comes to chairing meetings, there are a few pointers that can make the whole process relatively pain-free!

○ Make sure that there is an agenda and that minutes are taken.
○ Ask for items for the agenda or put up a noticeboard so that any 'hot topics' can be raised.
○ Be realistic about what can be achieved in the time slot.
○ Make sure the meetings start and end on time.
○ Be ruthless and business-like about sticking to the agenda.
○ Consider having a revolving chairperson so that all staff members gain experience of running a meeting.
○ Encourage everyone to participate – if the issue is important and will affect staff, make sure that everyone has their say.
○ Do not allow particular people to dominate the meeting – once they have made their point, thank them and then invite other contributions.
○ Do not expect staff to participate if the meetings are held in unpaid time. If staff meetings are part of the job, staff should understand that they are being paid for this time.
○ Never have a meeting just for the sake of it.

Working with assistants and volunteers

LIST 88

Assistants and volunteers can provide great support in settings. Sadly though, their talents are not always recognized.

Starting points

○ Greet any helpers with enthusiasm.
○ Remember to thank them for their support and time.
○ Don't expect them to work things out for themselves – a little investment in time from you will help them quickly to gain skills and expertise.
○ Make sure that you plan interesting tasks for them – no one wants to feel like a slave.

Getting the best from your helpers

○ Find out what their skills and interests are.
○ Find out what attracted them to working in the setting and build on this when planning tasks.
○ Provide constructive feedback so that they can build their confidence.
○ Look for areas where they can develop their skills, e.g. becoming experts at helping children to paint.
○ Consider giving them the same children to work with – developing a relationship with a group of children is more rewarding than washing out paint pots!
○ Invite them to attend training courses.
○ Make sure that they understand the policies for child protection, confidentiality and behaviour.
○ Finally, remember that volunteers can vote with their feet. If you started with five parent helpers but within a few weeks have none, you are doing something wrong!

LIST 89 Using students effectively

Students on placement or on work experience can be a fantastic support when we need an extra pair of hands. But in order for us and them to get the most out of their stay, it is important that we use them effectively.

Before they arrive find out:

- which course they are on, the level and how much experience they have
- whether they have to do any activities or observations during their time with you
- what time they should leave and arrive
- if there are any reports or documentation that you need to fill in
- who you should contact if the student does not turn up or is seriously bad!

When the student arrives:

- smile and greet them
- take time to show them around and explain what they will be doing
- explain any of the quirks of your setting, e.g. 'in the staffroom, don't ever use the mug with a dog on it – Kath will go mad!'
- make sure that they understand about child protection, confidentiality and behaviour
- take things slowly but make sure that they do get to work with children!
- encourage them to ask questions.

Do:

- remember that they may be nervous and also inexperienced
- praise and give them positive feedback.

Don't:

- expect them to remember everything that they are told – write some of it down

- give them all the repetitive tasks, such as cleaning out the stock cupboard
- leave them alone with individual or groups of children
- take students unless you are prepared to invest some time in training them.

Preparing for inspection

The trend for inspections is to provide little or no notice. The idea is to take the stress out of the inspection process!

Getting everything together

○ Create an inspection box and put inside it:
  - information about your setting – this could be the prospectus
  - all policies and documentation
  - a folder containing positive feedback from parents, e.g. cards and notes that have been sent
  - back and current copies of planning documents
  - a folder showing training that staff have undertaken
  - records of staff meetings to date
  - the development plan
  - a contents list.
○ Make sure that everyone in the setting knows where the box is kept.
○ Where items such as the accident book or registers are kept elsewhere, make sure everyone knows where they can be found.

LIST 91   Keeping up the standards

It is important not just to prepare for inspection, but also to put into place systems so that standards can be maintained. Check that the place where you work is doing some or all of the following:

❍ Auditing the setting from time to time – identifying weaknesses and strengths, and devising a development plan from these audits.

❍ Keeping agendas and minutes of all staff meetings.

❍ Keeping staff appraisal forms up to date.

❍ Creating and monitoring a system to check that children's records are maintained.

❍ Dedicating a small slot at each staff meeting to one curriculum area or policy.

❍ Providing an up-to-date curriculum or framework folder for each area.

❍ Ensuring that planning is done by the people who will be working with the children.

❍ Avoiding situations where only one person knows what is meant to be happening.

❍ Sending out satisfaction and feedback forms to parents at least once a year and collating them to provide evidence of parental satisfaction. On the inspection day, the inspectors will otherwise base their views on those parents they meet!

Coping with inspection

The doorbell rings and suddenly the inspector has arrived!

○ Smile and make sure that you feel calm and relaxed.

○ Be encouraging to other staff.

○ If you know of areas where there are weaknesses, consider launching a pre-emptive strike. It is always better to come clean rather than wait for the inspector to discover what is awry.

○ Be ready to ask questions as to how the inspection will take place.

○ Have any documentation and evidence to hand – make sure that you give it to the inspector.

○ Keep an eye out for colleagues who are not coping well.

After the inspection process

○ Immediate feedback is now given after an inspection, before the report is written.

○ Remain courteous and polite.

○ Listen carefully to everything that is said – don't focus only on criticisms.

○ Challenge anything that you feel is unfair and use other sources of information, such as the curriculum document, as evidence.

○ Find out if any supplementary evidence is needed, such as planning that shows that children do play outdoors, even if this was not seen on the day.

○ If you feel that the inspection process has been unfair, it is possible to appeal directly to the inspectorate. Use the relevant website to find out more.

○ Finally, relax and have a big party, regardless of the outcome!

Moving On | 11

LIST 93 — Making the most of training

Few people these days can say that they have a job for life. So, even if you are feeling quite settled, you should keep up to date with your professional skills and knowledge as you never know when you might want or need to move on.

Choosing training

- ○ Think strategically. What areas of your professional development need working on or brushing up? What skills are in demand in the sector?
- ○ Look out for courses that can lead to a qualification. This is really important if you qualified a long time ago or if you think that your current level of qualification will not be sufficient to gain a promotion.

Where to look for training

- ○ Early years and School Improvement services.
- ○ Local colleges of FE.
- ○ Universities – many offer part-time and distance learning courses.
- ○ The Open University.
- ○ Training sections in early years magazines such as *Nursery World* and *Early Years Educator*.

Funding

- ○ Many employers will fund your training if they can see that it is in their interests to do so, but do check whether there are any strings attached, such as refunding the cost if you leave within six months!
- ○ Bursaries and grants from early years services, universities and colleges.

Keeping a record of training

○ Prepare a training folder for yourself. Include:
- dates of any training you have attended, including in-house training
- certificates of attendance
- notes and handouts.

Creating opportunities

Some people seem to have all the luck when it comes to their careers, but really it's all about making the most of the opportunities that come your way.

○ Think long term – don't expect immediate promotion or pay.
○ Be positive – see any new development in planning and organization as an opportunity to gain new skills.
○ Look out for training opportunities.
○ Take additional qualifications.
○ Volunteer for projects and roles that will help you meet people outside your setting – press officer, liaison with child protection team.
○ Become an NVQ assessor.
○ Work with different ages of children within your setting – don't get stereotyped.
○ Do some work experience in other areas of the sector, such as out-of-school clubs or hospitals.

You may be good at working with children, but can you also offer an employer something else?

○ Financial administration – book-keeping, payroll, budgeting.
○ Special educational needs – behaviour management skills, becoming a SENCO.
○ Management – a qualification in management.
○ ICT – building a website, using ICT with children or as a tool for curriculum planning.
○ Project management – setting up or extending services, such as a breakfast club, out-of-school club, advertising, marketing, finding funding.
○ Health and safety – a qualification in health and safety.

Networking effectively

Most early years settings are quite small and it is easy to miss out on what is happening in the big world. Networking is about building up professional contacts.

Why network?

- To meet other professionals and have a collective moan!
- To find out about other job opportunities.
- To make friends – especially if you are new to an area.
- To share experiences, tips and ideas.
- To get help and support.

Where can I network?

- Join a 'cluster' group – these are common in many areas and are usually organised by local early years services. They usually meet at the end of the day.
- Conferences – most areas hold at least one early years conference a year.
- Courses and training days.
- Liaison meetings – look out for meetings of SENCOs, child protection agencies.

How to network

- Talk to someone! Look out for someone who is looking equally unsure, smile and ask where they are from and what they do. Make an effort to remember their name!
- Don't slag off your colleagues or where you work – you never know, you might be talking to a friend of the manager!
- Aim to meet someone new each time you attend an event – avoid becoming part of a 'mafia' when you are with colleagues.
- Keep a professional contact book – put down names of people, their role and where they work.

Where to look for a job

It is good idea to keep an eye on what's on offer, even if you are reasonably settled in your job. It is also important to remember that few people get offered their dream job – they usually have to find it!

○ Magazines such as *Nursery World*.
○ *The Times Educational Supplement*.
○ Local newspapers.
○ Employment agencies – look out for ones that specialize in early years and teaching.
○ Early years teams – many early years advisors will know which nurseries and schools have vacancies or are expanding.
○ Jobcentre – not a brilliant bet, but still worth exploring.
○ Websites – if you know who you want to work for, see if they have a vacancies section on their website.
○ Word of mouth – if you have built up your professional networks, you might come to hear of a job this way.
○ Be direct – don't be afraid to make direct contact with an employer. Phone up and ask to speak to the personnel section or the manager. Express an interest in working for them. Offer to send in a CV or better still drop one off in person.

How to get an interview

○ Apply for the post quickly – if your application is the first or second, it is bound to be read and remembered.

○ Do exactly what the advert says – if it says write for an application pack, don't phone or call in (it's hardly a good start if an applicant can't follow simple instructions).

○ Photocopy the application form so that you have a spare one if you make a mistake.

○ Read the job description carefully – this is what you would be signing up to do.

○ Read the person specification – make sure that you can meet the 'essential requirements' list.

○ Think about whether or not you really want the job – research the organisation a little!

○ Make sure that your CV or application shows how you meet the person specification and will be able to meet the job description.

○ Be accurate and avoid exaggeration – explain any gaps in your employment record.

○ Ask your 'potential' referees if they will give you a reference before putting them down.

○ Pop in a short covering note on good quality plain stationery – something such as 'Please find enclosed my application for "x" post. May I thank you for considering me...' Use your best handwriting!

LIST 98 Preparing for interviews

Preparation is the key for a good interview. Don't assume that it will all just fall into place on the day.

- Read through the job description and person specification carefully.
- Highlight the main skills and qualities that are required.
- Think about how you can show that you have them or will acquire them.
- Consider the questions you are likely to be asked (see List 99).
- Find out more about the setting – use inspection reports, prospectus, website.
- Think about what you will be able to offer, for example, a setting whose Ofsted report suggested that there was a weakness with outdoor play will be pleased with someone who tells them that they love outdoor play!

Practical matters

- Book time off from your employer.
- Work out how long it will take you to get there on the day and carry out a dummy run. Think about a plan B if it rains, the bus is late or the car won't start.
- Read through the letter inviting you for an interview carefully as a basis for deciding what to wear. If you have to work with children, choose practical clothes.
- Check that your suit/skirt/outfit still fits several days before! Ask an honest friend who is good at presenting themselves what they think!

Answering questions at interviews

○ *Tell me about yourself.* This can be an introductory question. It is a key opportunity to make a good impression and to sell yourself. Prepare carefully for this question with at least three or four good points, such as how long you have been working with children, your strengths and skills and even why you want this job.

○ *What are your strengths?* This is another ideal opportunity to sell yourself. Think about the person specification when preparing for this question. What was the employer looking for? Use phrases such as 'I feel that I am' to avoid seeming arrogant. Don't exaggerate or lie!

○ *What are your weaknesses?* Do not tell your future employer all your bad habits! Instead, think of one or two areas in which you could do with more experience or skills. Then go on to explain how you intend to work on them – 'I feel that my ICT skills are a weak point, but I am going to enrol on a course later this year.'

○ *Why are you interested in this post?* Extra holidays and pay are not good answers! Try to talk about the extra experience or new challenges that the post will bring.

○ *What do you feel you can bring to the post?* Another question which will allow you to sell yourself! Think about your experience, maturity, enthusiasm or ability to work with others, but make sure your answer corresponds with the person specification.

LIST 100   Top tips for a good interview

Keeping calm on the day of the interview will make a lot of difference. Try out these tips.

- Get out the letter and check the time of the interview.
- Read through the prospectus and job description again.
- Get there ten minutes before the interview begins – do not arrive any earlier as you may just clutter up the place.
- Be polite to everyone you meet – the trend to dress down may mean that someone you mistake for the cleaner is really the manager!
- Look for ways of complimenting what is happening in the setting, such as the displays, the conduct of children.
- Cut down on clutter, and keep bags or coats to the minimum – avoid looking like a 'bag lady'.
- Pop to the loo and do a final hair and make-up check if required.
- Think carefully before accepting food or drinks – if you are nervy, you may end up spilling them or being asked a question when you've got your mouth full. If you're invited to lunch, remember to polish up your table manners.
- Remember that first impressions count at interview – smile as you go in, make eye contact and, if you can, offer a quick handshake. Look calm!
- Listen carefully to the questions – if you do not understand a question, say so.
- If needed, buy some time before responding to tricky questions – use phrases such as 'That's an interesting question.' If you are really bold, say that you need a moment to reflect. This puts you in a good light as it shows that you are not impulsive.
- Avoid rambling – once you have finished answering a question, bring your voice down to a 'full stop'.
- Sound enthusiastic – this counts for a lot and can make up for any 'goofs'.
- Avoid asking questions that are not relevant or that you should already know the answer to.
- When the interview has ended, thank the interviewer for their time. Offer to shake hands – final impressions can make a difference too!

And if you don't get the job...

○ Think about asking for feedback. If you can bear to do so, listen carefully to what is being said.

○ Do not question their judgement or tell them that you didn't want the job anyway!

LIST 101 Considering your options

The early years sector is an expanding one. There are many directions that you can travel in providing you are ready to have a go! Think about your present job and the elements that you enjoy and that give you satisfaction. With a bit of lateral thinking you'll be able to apply your skills to other areas.

About you

- What are your strengths and weaknesses?
- How much contact do you want to have with children?
- Do you enjoy 'hands on' work or administration?
- Are you prepared to study for a further qualification?
- Would you consider being a volunteer in order to gain valuable experience?
- Have you an interest that you could develop further, e.g. working with parents?
- Would you consider a drop in salary over a short-term period?
- Have you made contacts with anyone working in this area?
- Could you get another post easily, if it didn't work out?

Other jobs to consider

- Play worker
- Development officer
- Early-years adviser
- Regional manager for nursery chains
- Education consultant
- Early-years trainer
- Educational psychologist
- Children's centre manager
- Educational welfare officer.